THE
DUCK SOUP
GUITAR METHOD

Beginning Guitar With Super-Easy Chords

HARVEY REID

WOODPECKER
MULTIMEDIA

York, Maine USA

Music copy: Jeff Hickey
Design & Graphics: Aphro-Graphics

The *Duck Soup Guitar Method* was developed by guitarist Harvey Reid in 1980 and first published in 1982. Special thanks to Terry Kuhn, Jeff Hickey and Lyle Shabram.

The Third Hand Capo is a trademark of Woodpecker Multimedia and is protected by U.S. patent # 4183279

ISBN: 978-1-63029-000-9
Library of Congress Control# 2013951624

WOODPECKER
MULTIMEDIA

PO Box 815 York Maine 03909 USA

www.woodpecker.com

CONTENTS

What is *Duck Soup Guitar*™?

It's totally new and unique...
For centuries, beginners have faced the same guitar chords, that are actually somewhat daunting to master, even though everyone says it is easy to play them. Finally, after 400 years, there really is an easier way. All sorts of guitarists are using partial capos to play fancy guitar and to write and arrange songs with new sounds. And they are very helpful to beginners also.

It yields immediate results...
Quite simply, it works. Almost anyone can strum full-sounding guitar chords instantly, with no skills, knowledge or practice.

It requires no previous musical knowledge...
You don't need to know how to read music. All you do is start strumming the one-finger guitar chords and you'll be singing along with all the songs in this book right away. Everything you need to know about strumming, tuning, singing and following the songs is right here. It's just "campfire guitar" made much easier.

It's a perfect way to start playing the guitar...
You'll develop your rhythm and strumming skills, left-hand chording, and confidence as you sing these familiar songs. The skills are sequenced in a natural progression, so that when you finish *Duck Soup Guitar* you'll be ready for "conventional" guitar programs.

It makes learning to play guitar easy and fun...
If you've always wanted to play guitar, this is the time to start. All you need is a guitar, a *partial capo*, and this book. There's no frustration, and nothing complicated to do. It is so easy to do that you'll be able to enjoy making music and singing along right from the very first song. It's *Duck Soup*. (Which means it's easy and fun.)

The Problem: Easy Guitar Is Still Too Hard

The biggest challenge in beginning guitar is that it takes even a motivated adult months of effort before they can play the simplest chords to accompany songs. Even the most basic guitar chords require 3 and 4 fingers of the left hand.

Millions of people can't get going playing recreational "campfire" guitar because it's just a bit too hard to do. It takes a surprising amount of time and considerable dexterity just to learn some chords to accompany basic songs.

This book shows several new ways to simplify basic chords, so that beginners can play great-sounding simple songs with just 1 or 2 fingers and have a "success experience."

Other short-cut methods that use open tunings have a lot of limitations, since you aren't learning in standard tuning, and chord options are very limited.

BASIC CHORDS IN STANDARD TUNING

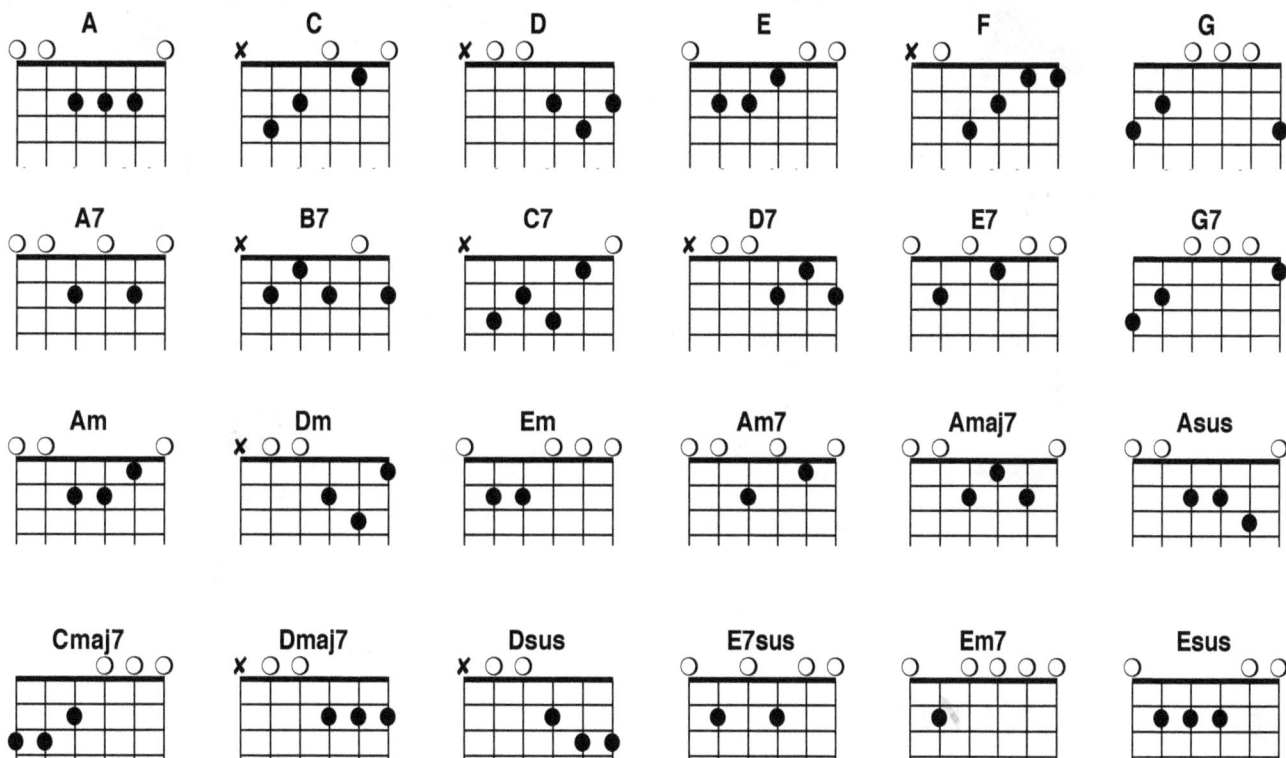

A C D E F G

A7 B7 C7 D7 E7 G7

Am Dm Em Am7 Amaj7 Asus

Cmaj7 Dmaj7 Dsus E7sus Em7 Esus

Teachers often steer beginning students into playing instrumental single-note guitar, since chords are too hard at first, and there may be only a feeling of frustration and no progress. Single-note guitar appears to make sense; it is a logical, step-by-step approach, and it feels like you are learning music, but it has a very high drop-out rate, and is not really "recreational." Instrumental guitar is difficult, and offers little reward to casual beginners who only want to play some campfire-style guitar to accompany songs.

Web sites, beginner guitar books and videos that emphasize how easy it is to play guitar have actually created an extra psychological barrier, causing even more beginners to give up and blame themselves for being un-musical or un-motivated because they expect it to be as easy as all the ads say it is. The truth is that beginning guitar chords take a surprising amount of time to master, and only a small percentage of those who start ever get to the point where they can actually play a song.

👉 THE PARTIAL CAPO

The **Duck Soup Guitar**™ method makes use of a recent guitar innovation called a partial capo. Capos have existed for centuries, clamping across the guitar strings to raise the pitch of all the strings at once, usually used to suit a singer's voice. The *Third Hand Capo* and the *Spider Capo* allow you to clamp any combination of strings. The *Shubb c7b* and the *Kyser Short Cut* are both single-purpose partial capos that also allow you to play songs in the *Duck Soup Guitar* book, though not in as many ways. Partial capos are often used by accomplished guitarists as a way to expand the musical possibilities of the instrument, but they also give a beginner a way to enjoy full-sounding guitar music immediately. Learn more about all kinds of partial capos at *www.PartialCapo.com*. They are useful for all levels of players.

Third Hand Capo (Universal)

Shubb c7b Capo (Esus/A)

Kyser Short Cut Capo (Esus/A)

Liberty "Flip" Capo

SpiderCapo (Universal)

👉 TUNING

It is important that your guitar be in tune, at least with itself, and hopefully with the established pitches of a guitar. The easiest way to get your guitar in tune is to find someone who knows how to do it, and have them do it for you. It only takes a minute when you know how, and it's not that hard to learn. Here are some methods you can use.

Electronic tuners You can purchase an electronic device that will tell you when each string is in tune. This is easy, and very accurate, though tuners need batteries, and can be hard to use in a noisy environment.

Tuning to another instrument The correct pitches of each string with the capo attached in each configuration used in this book are shown in the keyboard diagrams below. Remember: The guitar remains in standard or 'concert' tuning throughout this book. Be sure to put the capo on before tuning to these pitches.

4

In E suspended capo configuration

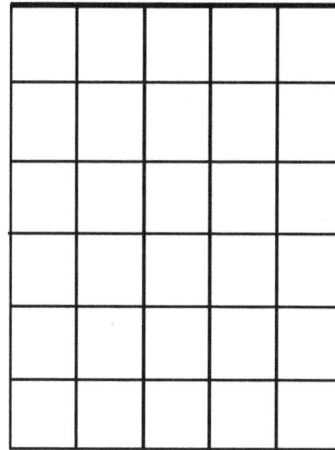

middle C

In Easy C capo configuration

In Open A capo configuration

E A D G B E

The strings of the guitar

BASS   **TREBLE**

Tuning to a reference note This is probably the most commonly used method. Use a pitch pipe or tuning fork, another instrument, or any other method (a telephone dial tone is a perfect F) to tune one string, then tune the other strings to it using one of the following rules:

The black dots on the diagrams indicate where to fret each string to produce the proper pitch for the next higher (thinner) string.

No capo   Esus   Open A   Easy C

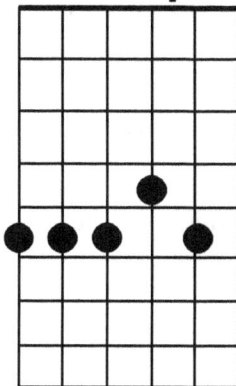
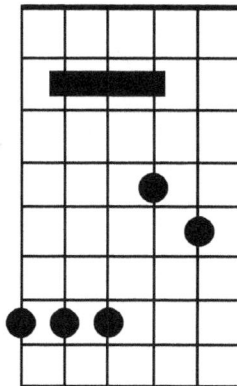
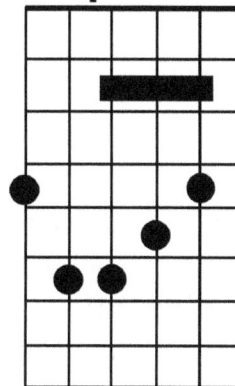
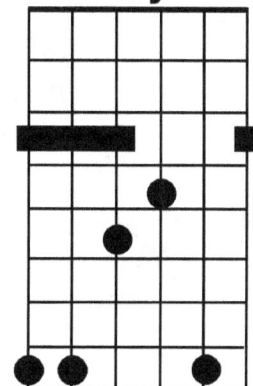

When you switch from one configuration of a partial capo to another, you will probably have to slightly re-adjust the tuning of some of the strings. This is normal. If the guitar sounds OK to you, it is probably in tune. If someone complains that it is not in tune, then have them help you tune it.

👉 E SUSPENDED

This book employs the easy, full-sounding chords shown below, when the partial capo is placed to form what is called an Esus or E suspended chord. We will call them **I = ONE, IV = FOUR, and V = FIVE** chords, which are standard terms used in music theory. These chords shown here function as E, A and B7 chords (They are actually E^5, **Aadd9** and **B7sus** chords) and are the primary chords for the key of E major. The last two sections in this book show how to play easy chords in the keys of A major and C major.

I

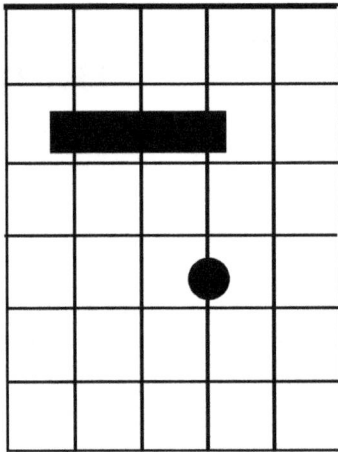

"E"

IV

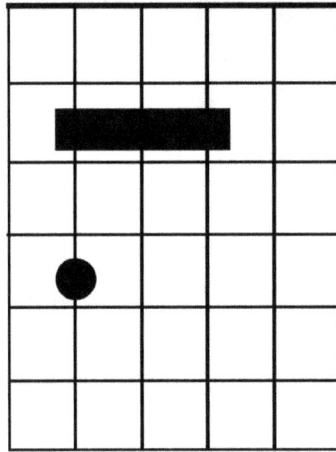

"A"

V

X

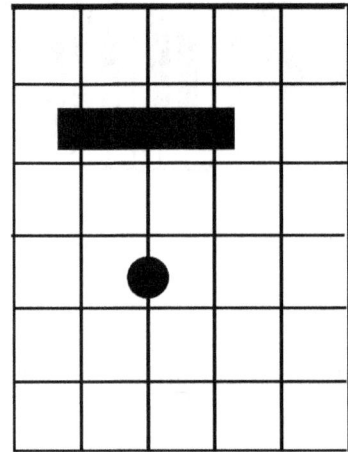

"B7"

Reading the chord diagrams– The vertical lines represent the strings, with the bass (thicker) strings on the left. The horizontal lines represent the frets of the guitar. The round dots tell you where to place your fingers, while the rectangles show the position of the capo. The X above the string in the diagram indicates if that string is not to be strummed with the strumming hand.

Hints on playing– Use the tip of your finger to fret the string, and try to avoid touching adjacent strings. Your finger should be just behind the metal fret, and you should apply enough pressure to obtain a clear tone from each string. Use whichever finger seems most comfortable.

☛ STRUMMING

Strumming a guitar is like tapping your foot with your arm. You have to hit the strings in time with the music. You can use your thumb, fingers, guitar pick, or any object like a piece of plastic or even cardboard. You can strum with a 'downstroke' (toward the floor) or an 'upstroke.' Different combinations of downstrokes and upstrokes can create different kinds of rhythms for different kinds of folks, so feel free to experiment, and to do what feels natural. There is no 'correct' way to strum, and the best way for you is the one that feels best to you. Sing the song and tap your foot. Each time you tap your foot is called a 'beat.' Most common rhythm patterns involve beat groupings of 2, 3, 4, 6 or 8 beats. The beat grouping is shown at the beginning of each song in written music as the upper number or numerator of 2 numbers on the musical staff, known as the "time signature." In 4/4 time, each beat grouping, called a 'measure' or 'bar', contains 4 beats. The lower number indicates what type of note gets one beat, with 4 being a 'quarter note.' The first beat of each measure is usually accented (louder.) Tap your foot at a steady pace and count:

ONE- 2 3 4 / ONE-2 3 4 / ONE- 2 3 4 etc.

Strum once for each beat, stressing the ONE beat of each measure. The speed of the beats is called the 'tempo.' There is nothing wrong with simply strumming once per beat; however strumming twice per beat (down/up or D/U) on certain beats and not strumming at all on others can create interesting and quite musical rhythms. Here are some common examples of rhythm strumming patterns, which you can use for most of the songs in this book.

	3/4 TIME					
Count	1	2	3	1	2	3...
Strum	D	D	D	D	D	D
Count	1	2 and	3 and	1	2 and	3 and
Strum	D	D/U	D/U	D	D/U	D/U
Count	1	2	3 and	1	2	3 and
Strum	D	D	D/U	D	D	D/U
Count	1 and	2 and	3 and	1 and	2 and	3 and
Strum	D/U	D/U	D/U	D/U	D/U	D/U

	4/4 TIME						
Count	1	2	3	4	1	2	3	4...
Strum	D	D	D	D	D	D	D	D
Count	1	2	3	4 and	1	2	3	4 and
Strum	D	D	D	D/U	D	D	D	D/U
Count	1	2 and	3	4 and	1	2 and	3	4 and
Strum	D	D/U	D	D/U	D	D/U	D	D/U
Count	1	2	3	4	1	2	3	4...
Strum	D		D		D		D	faster songs

☞ PLAYING

Turn to the first song in this book. *Go Tell Aunt Rhody* is in 4/4 time, so each measure gets 4 beats. The Roman numeral above the staff tells you what chord to play. Just strum the beats, sing the song, and change the chord whenever a different Roman numeral appears. The songs at the beginning of the book have only two chords, while the later songs have three.

☞ HINTS ON SINGING

The songs in this book have been chosen so that the singing pitch is comfortable for most people. However, if the pitch is too low, you can raise it by placing a standard capo (or a *Third Hand* with all 6 discs down) on the guitar neck. The first partial capo should be moved up the neck an equal number of frets. The chart below shows how the pitch of the songs can be raised for keys other than E.

Standard Capo	Partial Capo (Esus)	Key
1st fret	3rd fret	F
2nd fret	4th fret	F# or Gb
3rd fret	5th fret	G
4th fret	6th fret	G# or Ab
5th fret	7th fret	A
6th fret	8th fret	A# or Bb
7th fret	9th fret	B

Other partial capo configurations in the later sections of the book show how you can sing 3-chord songs in some keys other than E.

☞ NOTATION

Although you will be playing the chords indicated by the Roman numerals above the staff, the melodies of the songs have been written out for you in both standard musical notation and in guitar tablature. This is to help you find the proper singing pitches, and to enable you to learn the melodies if you are not familiar with them. Tablature shows the 6 strings of the guitar the way you look at them, with the bass (thickest) string represented by the bottom line, and the treble (thinnest) by the top line. The numbers on the lines indicate at which fret of that string the string should be pressed to produce the proper note. A zero indicates that this string is to be played unfretted or 'open.' To avoid confusion, the tablature in this book always has the partial capo shown to remind you that it is in place on the guitar. **Remember: the numbers in the tablature refer to the number of frets above the capo.** Remember also that tablature does not tell you the time duration of the notes. That information can be obtained from the standard notation.

AUNT RHODY

GO   TELL AUNT RHO - DY

GO   TELL AUNT RHO - DY   GO   TELL AUNT

RHO - DY THE OLD GRAY GOOSE IS DEAD

The one that she's been saving, the one that she's been saving
The one that she's been saving, to make a feather bed

She died in the millpond, she died in the millpond
She died in the millpond, standing on her head

The goslings are crying, the goslings are crying
The goslings are crying, because their mommy's dead

HUSH, LITTLE BABY

HUSH LIT-TLE BA - BY DON'T SAY A WORD

PA-PA'S GON-NA BUY YOU A MOCK-ING BIRD - IF THAT MOCK-ING

BIRD DON'T SING PA-PA'S GON-NA BUY YOU A DIA-MOND RING

And if that diamond ring is brass, Papa's going to buy you a looking glass
And if that looking glass gets broke, Papa's going to buy you a billy goat

And if that billy goat don't pull, Papa's going to buy you a cart and bull
And if that cart and bull turn over, Papa's going to buy you a dog named Rover

And if that dog named Rover don't bark, Papa's going to buy you a horse and cart
And if that horse and cart fall down, you'll still be the sweetest little baby in town

DOWN IN THE VALLEY

DOWN IN THE VAL - LEY THE VAL - LEY SO

LOW HANG YOUR HEAD O -

VER HEAR THE WIND BLOW

Hear the wind blow, love, hear the wind blow
Hang your head over, hear the wind blow

Roses are red, dear, violets are blue
Angels in Heaven know I love you
Know I love you, dear, know I love you
Angels in Heaven know I love you

Send me a letter, send it by mail
Send it in care of the Birmingham jail
Birmingham jail, love, Birmingham jail
Send it in care of the Birmingham jail

TOM DOOLEY

HANG DOWN YOUR HEAD TOM DOO - LEY

HANG DOWN YOUR HEAD AND CRY HANG DOWN YOUR HEAD TOM

DOO - LEY POOR BOY YOU'RE BOUND TO DIE

I met her on the mountain, there I took her life
I met her on the mountain, I stabbed her with my knife

About this time tomorrow, I reckon where I'll be
Down in some lonesome valley, hanging from an old oak tree

Hand me down my banjo, I'll pick it on my knee
Where I'll be tomorrow it'll be no use to me

LONDON BRIDGE

LON - DON BRIDGE IS FALL - ING DOWN

FALL - ING DOWN FALL - ING DOWN LON - DON BRIDGE IS

FALL - ING DOWN MY FAIR LA - DY

Build it up with iron bars, iron bars, iron bars
Build it up with iron bars, my fair lady

Iron bars will rust and break, rust and break,
    rust and break
Iron bars will rust and break, my fair lady

Build it up with bricks and stones, bricks and stones,
    bricks and stones
Build it up with bricks and stones, my fair lady

Bricks and stones will tumble down, tumble down, tumble down
Bricks and stones will tumble down, my fair lady

THE FARMER IN THE DELL

THE FAR - MER IN THE DELL THE

FAR - MER IN THE DELL HI HO THE

DER - RY-O THE FAR - MER IN THE DELL

The farmer chased the wife (2 times)
Hi ho the derry-o the farmer chased the wife

The wife chased the child (2 times)
Hi ho the derry-o the wife chased the child

The child chased the cat (2 times)
Hi ho the derry-o the child chased the cat

The cat chased the rat (2 times)
Hi ho the derry-o the cat chased the rat

The rat chased the cheese (2 times)
Hi ho the derry-o the rat chased the cheese

The cheese stands alone (2 times)
Hi ho the derry-o the cheese stands alone

The farmer in the dell (2 times)
Hi ho the derry-o the farmer in the dell

14

TEN LITTLE INDIANS

ONE LIT - TLE TWO LIT - TLE THREE LIT - TLE IN - DIANS

FOUR LIT - TLE FIVE LIT - TLE SIX LIT - TLE IN - DIANS SEVEN LIT - TLE EIGHT LIT - TLE

NINE LIT - TLE IN - DIANS TEN LIT - TLE IN - DIAN BOYS

Ten little nine little eight little Indians
Seven little six little five little Indians
Four little three little two little Indians
One little Indian boy

15

CLEMENTINE

OH MY DAR - LING OH MY DAR - LING OH MY

DAR - LING CLEM - EN - TINE YOU ARE LOST AND GONE FOR

EV - ER DREAD - FUL SOR - ROW CLEM - EN - TINE

In a cavern in a canyon excavating for a mine
Lived a miner, forty-niner, and his daughter Clementine

Drove she ducklings to the water every morning just at nine
Caught her foot against a splinter fell into the foaming brine

Like she was unto a fairy and her shoes were number nine
Herring boxes without topses, sandals were for Clementine

Ruby lips above the water blowing bubbles soft and fine
But alas I was no swimmer, so I lost my Clementine

How I missed her, how I missed her, how I missed my Clementine
Till I kissed her little sister, and forgot my Clementine

ROCK MY SOUL

ROCK MY SOUL IN THE BOS-OM OF A - BRA-HAM

ROCK MY SOUL IN THE BOS-OM OF A - BRA-HAM ROCK MY SOUL IN THE

BOS-OM OF A - BRA-HAM OH ROCK-A MY SOUL

So high I can't get over it (3 times)
Gotta go through the door

So low I can't get under it (3 times)
Gotta go through the door

So wide I can't get around it (3 times)
Gotta go through the door

BILLY BOY

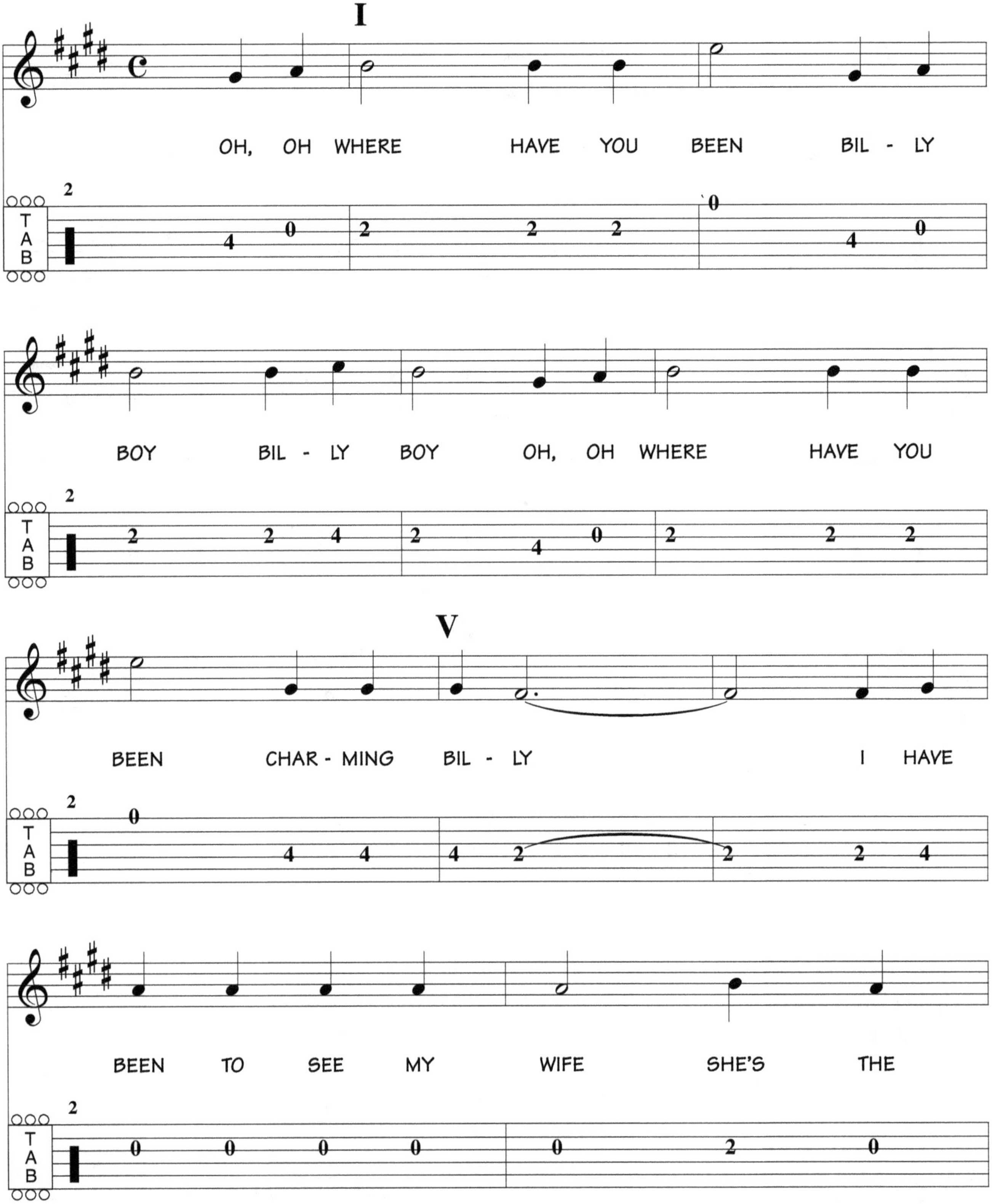

I

OH, OH WHERE HAVE YOU BEEN BIL - LY

BOY BIL - LY BOY OH, OH WHERE HAVE YOU

V

BEEN CHAR - MING BIL - LY I HAVE

BEEN TO SEE MY WIFE SHE'S THE

AP - PLE OF MY LIFE SHE'S A YOUNG THING AND

CAN - NOT LEAVE HER MO - THER

Did she bid you to come in, Billy Boy, Billy Boy?
Did she bid you to come in, charming Billy?
Yes she bid me to come in, there's a dimple in her chin
She's a young thing and cannot leave her mother

Can she bake a cherry pie, Billy Boy, Billy Boy?
Can she bake a cherry pie, charming Billy?
She can bake a cherry pie, quick as a cat can wink an eye
She's a young thing and cannot leave her mother

How old is she, Billy Boy, Billy Boy?
How old is she, charming Billy?
She's three times six and four times seven, twenty eight and eleven
She's a young thing and cannot leave her mother

STREETS OF LAREDO

AS I - WALKED OUT IN THE

STREETS OF LA - RE - DO AS I WALKED

OUT IN LA - RE - DO ONE DAY I

SPIED A YOUNG COW - BOY ALL

I   **V**   **I**

DRESSED   IN   WHITE   LI - N - EN   ALL   DRESSED   IN   WHITE

IV   **V**   **I**

LIN - EN   AND   COLD   AS   THE   CLAY

I see by your outfit that you are a cowboy
These words he did say as I boldly walked by
Come and sit down beside me and hear my sad story
For I'm shot in the breast and I know I must die

It was once in the saddle I used to go dashing
Once in the saddle I used to go gay
First down to Rosa's and then to the cardhouse
But I'm shot in the breast and I'm dying today

Get six sturdy cowboys to carry my coffin
Six pretty maidens to sing me a song
Put bunches of roses all over my coffin
For I'm a young cowboy and I know I've done wrong

Beat the drum slowly and play the fife lowly
Sing the dead march as you carry me along
Dig a hole in the prairie and lay the sod o'er me
I'm a young cowboy and I know I've done wrong

RED RIVER VALLEY

FROM THIS VAL - LEY THEY SAY YOU ARE

GO - ING WE WILL MISS YOUR BRIGHT

EYES AND SWEET SMILE FOR THEY

SAY YOU'LL BE TAK - ING THE SUN - SHINE

THAT HAS BRIGHT-ENED OUR   PATH - WAYS   A - WHILE

Come and sit by my side if you love me
Do not hasten to bid me adieu
Just remember the Red River Valley
And the girl [boy] who has loved you so true

SLOOP JOHN B

WE COME ON THE SLOOP JOHN B MY

GRAND - FA - THER AND ME 'ROUND NAUS - SAU

TOWN WE DID ROAM DRINK - ING ALL

NIGHT GOT IN-TO A FIGHT

The first mate he got drunk, broke in the captain's trunk
The constable had to come and take him away
Sheriff John Sloan why don't you leave me alone
I feel so broke up, I want to go home

So hoist up the John B sails
See how the mainsail sets
Call for the captain ashore let me go home
I want to go home, I want to go home
I feel so broke up, I want to go home

The poor cook he got the fits, ate up all of my grits
Then he took and he ate up all of my corn
Let me go home, I want to go home
This is the worst trip, I've ever been on

SHE'LL BE COMING 'ROUND THE MOUNTAIN

SHE'LL BE COM - ING 'ROUND THE MOUN-TAIN WHEN SHE

COMES   SHE'LL BE COM - ING 'ROUND THE

MOUN - TAIN WHEN SHE COMES   SHE'LL BE

COM - ING 'ROUND THE MOUN - TAIN SHE'LL BE

26

COM - ING 'ROUND THE MOUN - TAIN SHE'LL BE COM - ING 'ROUND THE

MOUN - TAIN WHEN SHE COMES

She'll be riding six white horses when she comes (2 times)
She'll be riding six white horses, she'll be riding six white horses
She'll be riding six white horses when she comes

We'll all *go down* to meet her when she comes (2 times)
We'll all *go down* to meet her, we'll all *go down* to meet her
We'll all *go down* to meet her when she comes

We'll all have chicken and dumplings when she comes (2 times)
We'll all have chicken and dumplings, we'll all have chicken and dumplings
We'll all have chicken and dumplings when she comes

AMAZING GRACE

BLIND   BUT   NOW   I   SEE

'Twas grace that taught my heart to fear, and grace my fears relieved
How precious did that grace appear, the hour I first believed

Must Jesus bear the cross alone, and all the world go free?
No, there's a cross for everyone, and there's a cross for me

Through many dangers, toils and snares, I have already come
'Twas grace has led me safe thus far, and grace will lead me home

When we've been here ten thousand years, bright shining as the sun
We've no less days to sing God's praise, as when we first begun

WORRIED MAN

I

IT TAKES A WOR - RIED MAN TO SING A WOR - RIED

IV

SONG IT TAKES A WOR - RIED MAN TO

I

SING A WOR - RIED SONG IT TAKES A WOR - RIED

MAN TO SING A WOR - RIED SONG I'M WOR - RIED

NOW   BUT I WON'T BE WOR-RIED LONG

I went 'cross the river and I laid down to sleep (3 times)
When I woke up, I had shackles on my feet

I asked the judge what's to be my fine (3 times)
Twenty one years on the Rocky Mountain Line

The train (that) I ride is twenty-one coaches long (3 times)
The girl I love is on that train and gone

If anyone should ask you, who wrote this song (3 times)
Tell 'em it was me and I sing it all day long

MICHAEL, ROW THE BOAT ASHORE

MI CHAEL ROW THE BOAT - A - SHORE HAL - LE -

LU - JAH MI - CHAEL ROW THE BOAT A -

SHORE HAL - LE - LU - U - JAH

Sister help me trim the sails
Hallelujah
Sister help me trim the sails
Hallelujah

River Jordan is chilly and cold
Hallelujah
Chills the body but not the soul
Hallelujah

River Jordan is deep and wide
Hallelujah
Got a home on the other side
Hallelujah

If you get there before I do
Hallelujah
Tell them all I'm coming too
Hallelujah

THIS OLD MAN

I   **IV**

THIS OLD MAN HE PLAYED ONE HE PLAYED KNICK KNACK

```
T  |  2     2   2     2   4   2   0       |
A  |     4            4              4    |
B  |                                      |
```

V   **I**

ON MY THUMB WITH A KNICK KNACK PAD-DY WHACK

```
T  |  2     0   4   0   2   0   0   0   0 |
A  |     4                                |
B  |                                      |
```

V   **I**

GIVE THE DOG A BONE THIS OLD MAN CAME ROL-LING HOME

```
T  |  0   2   4   0   2   2   2   2   0   4   2   0 |
A  |                                               |
B  |                                               |
```

This old man he played two, he played knick knack on my shoe...
This old man he played three, he played knick knack on my knee...
This old man he played four, he played knick knack on my door...
This old man he played five, he played knick knack on my hive...
This old man he played six, he played knick knack on my sticks...
This old man he played seven, he played knick knack till eleven...
This old man he played eight, he played knick knack on my gate...
This old man he played nine, he played knick knack on my spine...
This old man he played ten, he played knick knack over again...

LITTLE LIZA JANE

YOU GOT A GAL AND I GOT NONE   LIT - TLE   LI - ZA   JANE

COME HERE NOW AND   BE   MY ONE   LIT - TLE   LI - ZA   JANE

OH   E - LIZ - A   LIT - TLE   LI - ZA   JANE

OH   E - LIZ - A   LIT - TLE   LI - ZA   JANE

I've got a house in Baltimore
Little Liza Jane
Pretty girl sitting by my front door
Little Liza Jane
I've got carpets on my floor, Little Liza Jane

Who's that knockin' on my front door
Little Liza Jane

Come along and marry me, Little Liza Jane
We'll be happy wait and see, Little Liza Jane

OLD MACDONALD

OLD MAC-DON-ALD HAD A FARM EE - I - EE - I O AND
ON THIS FARM HE HAD A PIG EE - I - EE - I - O AN

OINK OINK HERE AN OINK OINK THERE HEREANOINKTHEREANOINKEVERY-WHEREAN OINKOINK

OLD MAC-DON-ALD HAD A FARM EE - I - EE - I - O

ducks...	with a	quack, quack here...etc.	cows...	with a	moo, moo here...etc.
turkeys...		gobble, gobble here...etc.	dogs...		bark, bark here...etc.
sheep...		baa, baa here...etc.	cats...		meow, meow here...etc.
horses..		neigh, neigh here...etc.			

SWING LOW, SWEET CHARIOT

SWING LOW   SWEET   CHA - RI - OT

COMING FOR TO CAR-RY ME HOME   SWING LOW   SWEET

CHA - RI - OT   COM-ING FOR TO CAR-RY ME HOME   I

LOOKED   O - VER JOR-DAN AND   WHAT   DID   I   SEE

I   **V**   **I**

COM-ING FOR TO CAR-RY ME HOME   A BAND   OF AN - GELS

IV   **I**   **V**   **I**

COM-ING AF-TER ME   COM-ING FOR TO CAR-RY ME   HOME

Some was crippled and some was lame
Coming for to carry me home
Still they came walking in my sweet Jesus' name
Coming for to carry me home

I don't know but I been told
Coming for to carry me home
Streets of Heaven are paved with gold
Coming for to carry me home

If you get there before I do
Coming for to carry me home
Tell all my friends I'm coming too
Coming for to carry me home

Sometimes I'm up and sometimes I'm down
Coming for to carry me home
Still my soul feels Heavenly bound
Coming for to carry me home

ANGELS WE HAVE HEARD ON HIGH

AN - GELS WE HAVE HEARD ON HIGH SWEET LY SING - ING

O'ER THE PLAIN AND THE MOUN - TAINS IN RE - PLY

EC - HO - ING THEIR GLAD RE - FRAIN GLOR - O-O-O-O-

OR - O-O-O-O-OR - O-O-O-O OR - I-A

IN EX - CEL - SIS DE - O GLOR - O - O - O - O -

OR - O - O - O - O - OR - O - O - O - O - OR - I - A

IN EX - CEL - SIS DE - E - O

Shepherds why this jubilee, why your joyous strains prolong?
What the gladsome tidings be, which inspire your heavenly song?

See him in the manger laid, whom the choirs of angels praise
Mary and Joseph lend you aid, while our hearts in love we raise

DECK THE HALLS

DON WE NOW OUR GAY AP - PAR - EL

FA LA LA LA LA LA LA LA LA TOLL THE AN - CIENT

YULE - TIDE CAR - OL FA LA LA LA LA LA LA LA LA

See the blazing Yule before us...
Strike the harp and join the chorus...
Follow me in merry measure...
While I tell of yuletide treasure...

Fast away the old year passes...
Hail the new ye lads and lasses...
Sing we joyous all together...
Heedless of the wind and weather

AULD LANG SYNE

SHOULD AULD AC - QUAIN - TANCE BE FOR - GOT AND

NEV - ER BROUGHT TO MIND SHOULD

AULD AC - QUAIN - TANCE BE FOR-GOT AND

DAYS OF AULD LANG SYNE FOR

42

I   V

AULD   LANG   SYNE   MY   FRIEND   FOR

I   IV   I

AULD   LANG   SYNE   WE'LL   TAKE   A   CUP   OF

V   IV   I

KIND - NESS   YET   FOR   AULD   LANG   SYNE

And here's a hand my trusty friend
And gie's a hand o' thine
We'll take a cup o' kindness yet
For auld lang syne

43

When you put the partial capo in the configuration shown below, you can play in the key of C, with new I, IV and V chords.

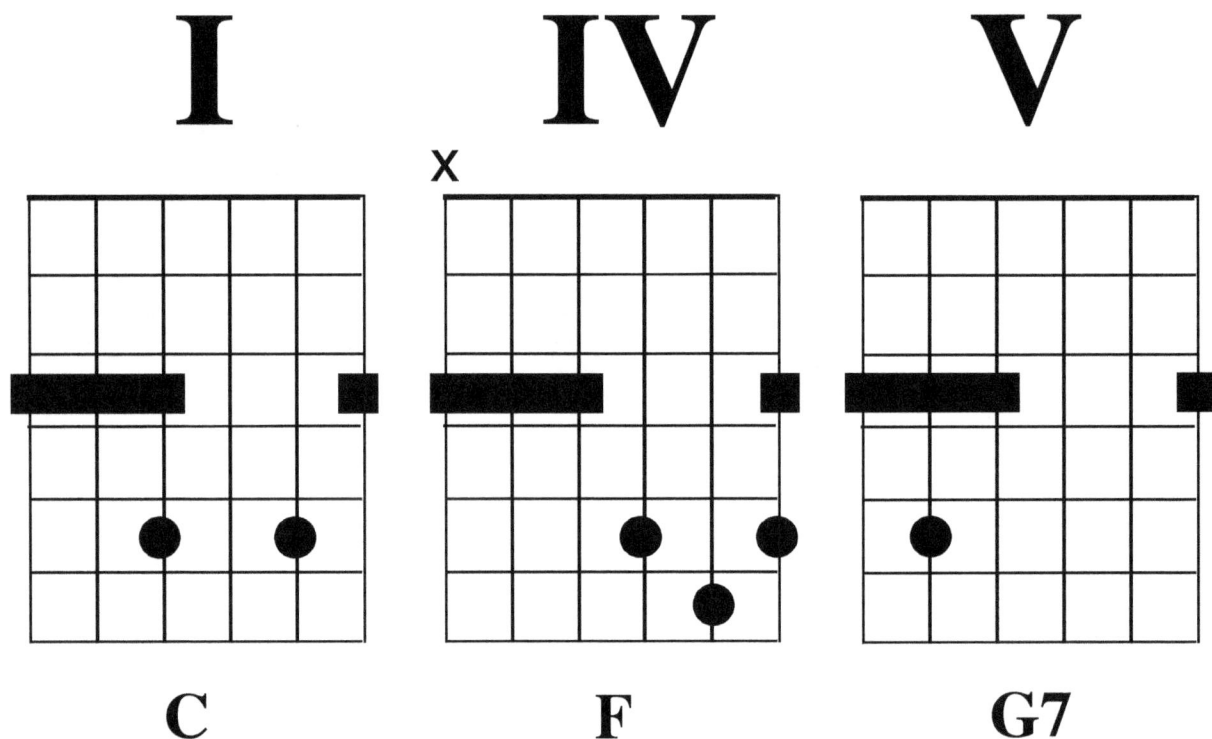

I   IV   V

C   F   G7

The songs in this book have been written with only I, IV, and V symbol for chords, so that it will be easy for you to switch and play the same songs in a different key and capo configuration. All you have to do is to substitute the new I, IV, and V chords in place of the old ones you were using in Esus, and sing the songs in a new key. You can find the singing pitches according to this rule: **The starting singing pitch of each song in Easy C is found on the next lower-pitched (thicker) string, at the same number of frets above the capo.** So *Aunt Rhody*, which starts on the 4th fret of the 4th or D string, starts on the 4th fret of the 5th or A string in Easy C.

The I, IV, and V chords in Easy C are actually real guitar chord forms without the capo. They form A7, D and Em7 (minor seventh) chords when you play them without a capo. In fact, many beginning guitar instruction books start with D and A7 chords, which are the I and V chords in the key of D. All the songs in this book that just use the I and V chords can be played in standard tuning without a partial capo. Although, when you use the capo, you can play 3 chord (I, IV, V) songs in the key of C just as easily. This configuration makes an ideal bridge into learning conventional guitar chords, and hopefully by the time you tackle the guitar chords that take 3 fingers, you will have already convinced yourself that playing guitar is easy, and have developed some skills and confidence.

SKIP TO MY LOU

I

FLY IN THE BUT-TER-MILK SHOO FLY SHOO

```
TAB
4   4  4  0  0  0   4   4         2
```

V   **I**

FLY IN THE BUT-TER-MILK SHOO FLY SHOO FLY IN THE BUT-TER-MILK

```
TAB
2  2  2        2  2      0   4  4  4  0  0  0
      4  4  4
```

V   **I**

SHOO FLY SHOO SKIP TO MY LOU MY DAR - LING

```
TAB
4   4     2     2   2   4   2   0      0
```

Lost my partner, what'll I do? (3 times)
Skip to my Lou my darling

I'll get another one, prettier than you (3 times)
Skip to my Lou my darling

Can't get a blue dress, a red one'll do (3 times)
Skip to my Lou my darling

SHENANDOAH

OH SHEN - AN - DOAH   I LONG TO

HEAR YOU   A   WAY

YOU ROL - LING RI - VER   OH

SHEN - AN - DOAH   I LONG TO HEAR YOU

Oh Shenandoah, I love your daughter
Away, you rolling river
Oh Shenandoah, I love your daughter
Away, I'm bound away, across the wide Missouri

Oh Shenandoah, I'm bound to leave you
Away, you rolling river
Oh Shenandoah, I'm bound to leave you
Away, I'm bound away, across the wide Missouri

OH, SUSANNAH

I

OH I COME FROM A - LA - BAM - A WITH MY

```
T
A    0    2    4         2         2         4    2         4    0         2
B
```

V   I

BAN - JO ON MY KNEE   I'M - A GOING TO LOU' - SI -

```
T
A    4    4    2    0         2         0    2    4    2         2         4
B
```

V   I

AN - A   MY   TRUE LOVE FOR   TO   SEE

```
T
A    2    4    0         2    4         4    2         2    0
B
```

IV   I   V

OH   SUS - AN - AH   OH ᐤON'T YOU CRY FOR ME   FOR I

```
T
A    0         0    4    4    4    2    2         4    0    2         0    2
B
```

48

It rained all night the day I left the weather it was dry
The sun so hot I froze myself, Susannah don't you cry

I had a dream the other night, when everything was still
I dreamed I saw Susannah, a coming down the hill
The buckwheat cake was in her mouth, the tear was in her eye
Says I "I'm coming from the South, Susannah don't you cry."

I soon will be in New Orleans, and then I'll look around
And when I find Susannah, I'll fall down on the ground.
And if I do not find her, then I will surely die
And when I'm dead and buried deep, Susannah don't you cry.

CAMPTOWN RACES

CAMP - TOWN LA - DIES SING THIS SONG DOO DAH

DOO DAH CAMP - TOWN RACE TRACK FIVE MILES LONG

OH THE DOO DAH DAY BOUND TO RUN ALL

NIGHT BOUND TO RUN ALL DAY I

BET MY MONEY ON A BOB-TAIL NAG SOME-BO-DY BET ON THE BAY

See those horses go around the bend, do-da, do-da
Guess that race will never end, oh the do-da day (chorus)

The long-tailed filly with the big black horse, do-da, do-da
They flew the track and they both cut across, oh the do-da day (chorus)

Blind horse stickin' in a big mud hole, do-da, do-da
Couldn't touch bottom with a ten-foot pole, oh the do-da day (chorus)

See them fly on a ten mile heat, do-da, do-da
Around the track and then repeat, oh the do-da day (chorus)

I win my money on the bobtail nag, do-da, do-da
I keep my money in an old tote bag, oh the do-da day (chorus)

☞ OPEN A

With the partial capo in the configuration shown below, songs can be played in the key of A with only slightly harder fingerings than in Esus. The I or A chord requires no left hand fingering at all! Be sure to avoid the 5th string when you play the V chord.

I   IV   V

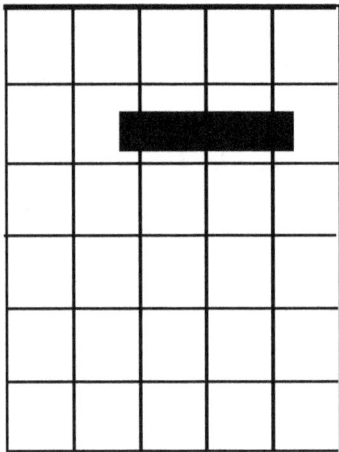
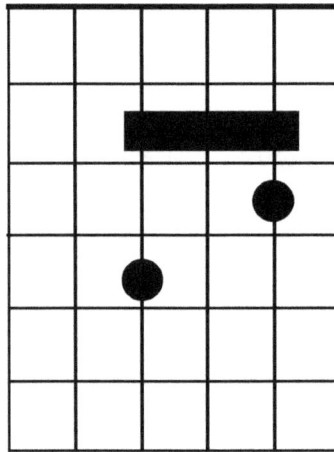
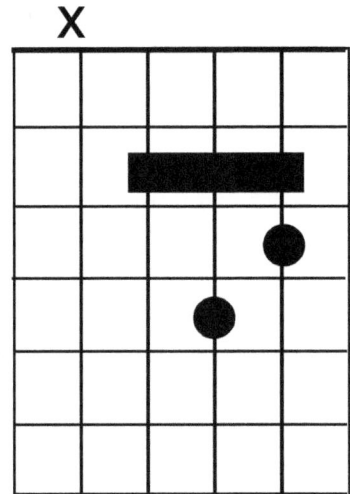

"A"   "D"   "E7"

All the songs in this book have been written with only I, IV and V symbols for chords, so that it will be easy for you to switch and play the same songs in a different key and capo configuration. If the song is not pitched right for your voice in E or C, try playing it in A using these chords. Just substitute the new I, IV and V chords in place of the old ones, and find the singing pitch according to this rule: **The pitch of each note in a song written in Esus (as most of them in this book are) will be 5 frets higher (closer to the body of the guitar) up the same string.** It will be 3 frets lower than the pitch of the notes for the songs written in Easy C.

When you play *Silent Night*, you will discover that although you will have to turn the page in the middle of the song, you will have a spare hand to do it, because the I chord you are playing at the time does not need your left hand!

SILENT NIGHT

Silent night, Holy night
Shepherds quake at the sight
Glories stream from Heaven afar
Heavenly hosts sing Hallelujah
Christ the Saviour is born
Christ the Saviour is born

Silent night, Holy night
Son of God, love's pure light
Radiant beams from thy holy face
With the dawn of redeeming grace
Jesus Lord at thy birth
Jesus Lord at thy birth

A Few More Ideas for Easy Chords...

All the songs in this book can be played with these three other sets of I, IV and V chords. They all have their advantages and disadvantages.

☞ "EASY E" CONFIGURATION

With a partial capo in same configuration as the Esus and the G string tuned down 1 fret to F#, all the songs in this book can be played in the key of E with slightly different fingerings and a slightly different sound. The E or I chord requires no left-hand fingering at all, and can allow a beginner to concentrate totally on strumming or other right-hand skills.

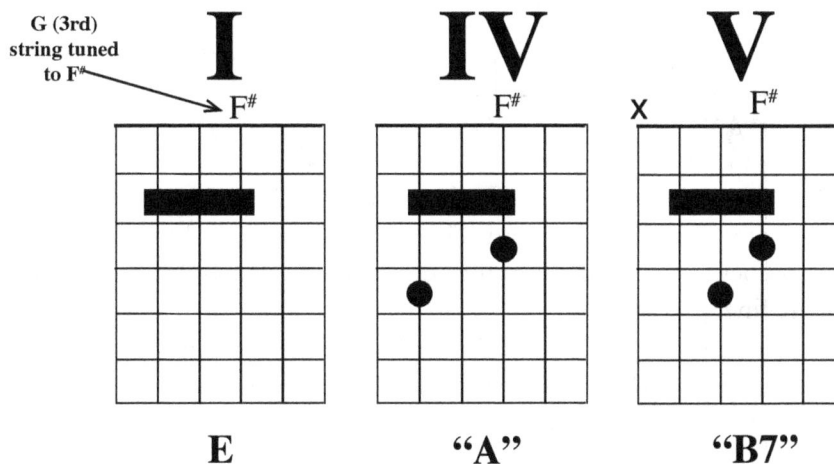

G (3rd)
string tuned
to F#

I	IV	V
F#	F#	x F#

E   **"A"**   **"B7"**

These 3 chords involve quite easy fingerings, though they have the same kinds of drawbacks as the capo configurations we looked at earlier.

• You have to avoid the 6th string when you play the V chord.

• The IV and V chords have some extra notes in them. The IV is an *Aadd9*, and the V is a *suspended 7th*. This sometimes makes them sound better, and sometimes they don't work as well on some songs. It's up to you: if you like the way they sound then they are fine. Many professionals and songwriters use these chords because they like the different sound.

• Since this is not standard tuning, the chord shapes used here are no longer just partial fingerings of standard guitar chords, and you can't use them later once you start playing "regular" guitar. This is a minor problem, since guitar playing is all about learning new fingerings.

• The *Easy E* configuration has a true E chord for its I chord, which means it has a G# note in it along with the E's and B's. The I chord in the Esus configuration is actually a "modal" chord which means it does not have a 3rd, and is made up of only E and B notes. For some songs the modal I is better, and for some songs it isn't. This Easy E configuration is a little confusing, but it does offer another easy way to play 3 chord songs, with some different musical options.

A SUSPENDED CONFIGURATION

With a partial capo as shown and the B string tuned up 1 fret to C, all the songs in this book can be played in the key of A with one finger, with slightly different fingerings than in either *Open A* or *Esus*. Since the open strings form an A suspended chord, this configuration is usually called *Asuspended* or *"Asus"* for short.

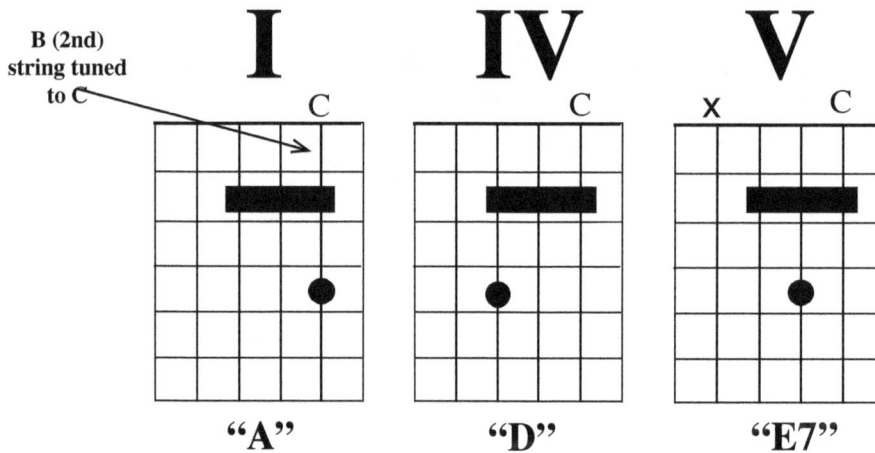

B (2nd) string tuned to C

I   IV   V

"A"   "D"   "E7"

• You have to avoid the 5th string when you play the V chord, which is hard for beginners.
• The IV and V chords have some extra notes in them. The IV is an *Aadd9*, and the V is a *suspended 7th*. This sometimes makes them sound better, and sometimes they don't sound as good. It's up to you: if you like the way they sound then they are fine.
• The *Open* A configuration has a true A chord for its I chord, which means it has a C# note in it along with the A's and E's. The I chord here in the *Asus* configuration is a "modal" chord which means it does not have a 3rd, and is made up of only A and E notes. For some songs the modal I is better, and for some songs it isn't.

ESUS @4 CONFIGURATION

With an *Esus* partial capo at fret 4, you can play 1, IV and V chords with a single 2-finger shape. The I chord is a "true" E chord, but the IV is an *Aadd9* and the V chord is a *B suspended*. They may sound fine to your ears or maybe not. Try them...

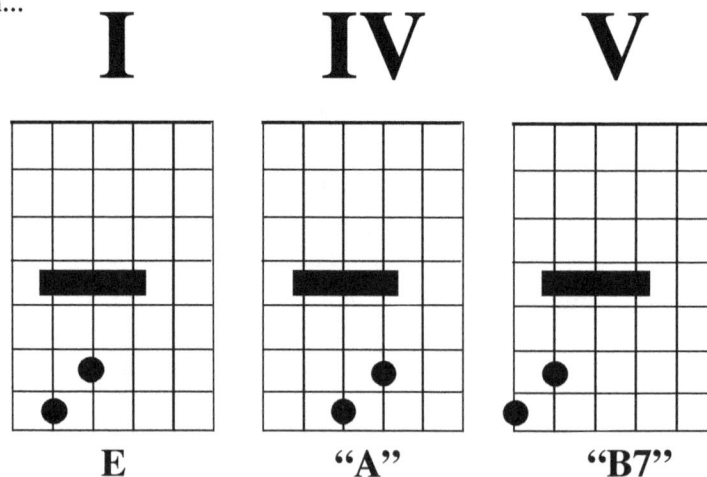

I   IV   V

E   "A"   "B7"

SOME POPULAR SONGS ALSO PLAYABLE WITH DUCK SOUP CHORDS

SONG	ARTIST
All I Really Want to Do	*Bob Dylan*
Amanda	*Waylon Jennings*
Back Home Again	*John Denver*
Blowing in the Wind	*Bob Dylan*
Blue Eyes Crying in the Rain	*Willie Nelson*
Both Sides Now	*Joni Mitchell*
Carrie	*Joni Mitchell*
Chimes of Freedom	*Bob Dylan*
Coat of Many Colors	*Dolly Parton*
Cold Cold Heart	*Hank Williams*
Deportees	*Woody Guthrie*
Dark As A Dungeon	*Merle Travis*
Early Morning Rain	*Gordon Lightfoot*
Faded Love	*Bob Wills*
The Gambler	*Kenny Rogers*
Good Hearted Woman	*Waylon Jennings*
Green Green Grass of Home	*Various Artists*
Guantanamera	*Various Artists*
Happy Birthday	*Everyone*
Hobo's Lullaby	*Arlo Guthrie*
I Can't Help It	*Hank Williams*
I'm So Lonesome I Could Cry	*Hank Williams*
Jambalaya	*Hank Williams*
Leaving On a Jet Plane	*Peter Paul & Mary*
Long Black Veil	*Various Artists*
Lucille	*Kenny Rogers*
King of the Road	*Roger Miller*
Last Thing on My Mind	*Tom Paxton*
Margaritaville	*Jimmy Buffett*
Me & Bobbie McGee	*Kris Kristofferson*
Mr Tambourine Man	*Bob Dylan*
Okie From Muskogee	*Merle Haggard*
Pack Up Your Sorrows	*Richard & Mimi Farina*
Paradise	*John Prine*
Peaceful Easy Feeling	*The Eagles*
Rambling Round	*Woody Guthrie*
She Thinks I Still Care	*George Jones*
This Land is Your Land	*Woody Guthrie*
Turn, Turn, Turn	*Pete Seeger*
Will the Circle Be Unbroken	*Carter Family*
You Are My Sunshine	*Jimmy Davis (+ many others)*

Due to copyright restrictions, the songs listed above cannot be included in this book. However, if you are teaching or learning guitar from Duck Soup Guitar, you will want to enrich your music program with some popular music. There are also many other popular songs you can play with just I, IV and V chords.

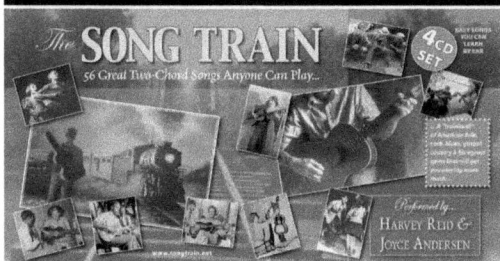

THE SONG TRAIN (2007) is a landmark resource for beginning guitarists by Harvey Reid & Joyce Andersen. 4-CD boxed set with 80-page color hardback book, contains 56 one & two chord songs. Half the songs are copyrighted, by the likes of Bob Dylan, Hank Williams, Chuck Berry etc, so it offers beginners easy but great songs they can play. Folk, blues, gospel, rock, celtic, country and gospel songs, and an amazing cross-section of American music. **www.songtrain.net**

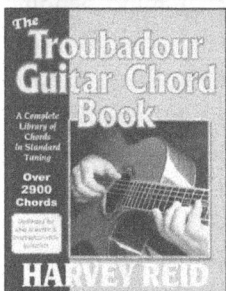

THE TROUBADOUR GUITAR CHORD BOOK (2013) The best, most complete and readable standard-tuning chord encyclopedia, and an essential new reference tool. A monumental and important new work that may never go back on your shelf. Unlike other large chord books that are tailored for jazz guitarists, the *Troubadour Guitar Chord Book* features over 2900 open and closed-string voicings, optimized and selected for solo acoustic and troubadour-style guitarists.

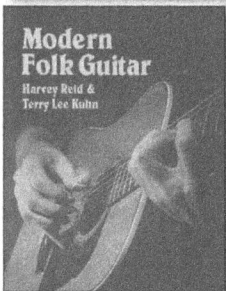

MODERN FOLK GUITAR (1984) The first college folk guitar textbook ever. A unique and comprehensive 325 page guitar handbook for the adult beginner, that has remained in print since 1984. It is used in the music departments of numerous universities to train music teachers. Many have called it the ultimate beginning folk guitar book. Scheduled to become a digital book in 2014.

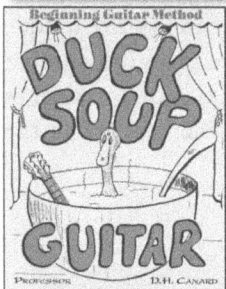

DUCK SOUP GUITAR: *Beginning Guitar With Super-Easy Chords* (1982) A little-known but revolutionary beginning guitar method. Shows how to use a partial capo to simplify guitar fingerings for beginners and people with special needs. Contains 28 children's songs with chords, notes & lyrics, and shows 6 clever ways to use a partial capo for easy chord fingerings. Anyone can play full-sounding guitar accompaniments instantly.

SLEIGHT OF HAND (1983) The first book of partial capo guitar arrangements, still in print. 16 solo guitar arrangements using a universal partial capo. Intermediate to advanced level, mostly for fingerstyle guitar, but has 2 flatpicked fiddle tune arrangements (*Sally Goodin'* and *Devil's Dream*) In TAB and standard notation. *Suite: For the Duchess, Für Elise, Scarborough Fair, Minuet in Dm, Flowers of Edinburgh, Simple Gifts, Sally Goodin', Irish Washerwoman, Pavanne, Minuet in Dm, Red-Haired Boy, June Apple, Jesu Joy of Man's Desiring, Devil's Dream, Sally Goodin', Scherzo, Shenandoah, Greensleeves, Sailor's Hornpipe, Fisher's Hornpipe*

CAPO INVENTIONS (2006) 16 intermediate to advanced arrangements from Reid's catalog of guitar recordings. Precisely transcribed for solo guitar, these pieces all use a 3-string *Esus* type partial capo. In TAB and standard notation. *Skye Boat Song, Highwire Hornpipe, Windy Grave, Hard Times, The Unknown Soldier, Suite: For the Duchess, The Arkansas Traveler, The Minstrel Boy, Red in the Sky, Prelude to the Minstrel's Dream, Norway Suite: Parts 1 &2, Star Island Jig, Macallan's Jig.*

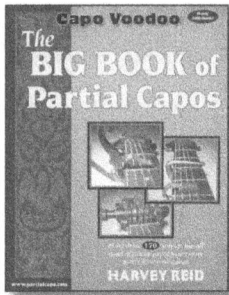

THE BIG BOOK OF PARTIAL CAPOS (2013) Finally a thorough and in-depth guide to the amazing world of partial capos. A colossal achievement and another landmark new resource by the partial capo pioneer, it takes you through almost 200 ways to use all types of partial capos, with over 6000 chords. Single and multiple partial capos, in standard tuning and combined with several dozen other tunings. Packed with photos, diagrams, strategy, advice and ingenious new ideas. Over 2/3 of these chords can't be played in standard tuning. For players of all levels and styles.

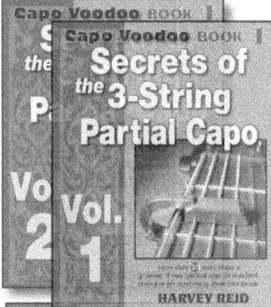

SECRETS OF THE 3-STRING PARTIAL CAPO VOL.1-2 A mind-bending number of ways to use the popular 3-string, Esus (*E-suspended*) partial capo. So many ideas it had to be split into 2 volumes! The "missing instructions" for the *Shubb* or *Kyser Esus* capos, this book shows you where to put the capo and where to put your fingers. (Also for *Third Hand* or *Spider* universal capos.) 2400 chords, crammed with tips, tricks, photos, advice, and ideas not available anywhere else. If you use an *Esus* capo, you need these books. Vol. 1 is standard tuning, and Vol. 2 uses one or more capos in other tunings.

SECRETS OF THE 4 & 5-STRING PARTIAL CAPOS Another treasure trove of ideas, for the *Planet Waves, Shubb,* or *Kyser* shortened 4 or 5-string capos. (Also valuable for *Third Hand, Liberty "Flip"* or *Spider* universal capos.) Most people who have one of these capos know a few ways to use them. Here are an amazing 47 ways to use a 4 or 5-string capo to find the new music hiding in every fingerboard. Over 1000 chords, together with a wealth of helpful information that appears nowhere else on Earth.

SECRETS OF THE 1 & 2-STRING PARTIAL CAPOS How to use the unique *Woodie's G-Band* 1 and 2-string partial capos. 33 clever ways to use these capos in a number of tunings and in combination with other partial capos, with over 1100 chords. 98 pages are packed with photos, ideas and capo knowledge that is only available here. Even the makers of the capos don't know about these ideas.

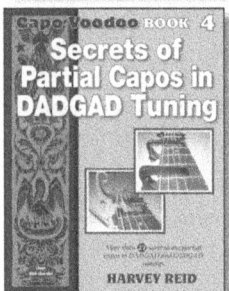

SECRETS OF PARTIAL CAPOS IN DADGAD TUNING Most people think of partial capos as a substitute for open tunings, and don't realize that they can be combined. Harvey Reid shows you over 25 ingenious ways to use partial capos to expand the musical possibilities of DADGAD tuning (4 of them use the similar CGDGAD tuning.) Get new chords, fingerings, voicings, resonances and unlock a new, mysterious world of new music hiding in your fingerboard. If you use DADGAD tuning a lot, you need this book.

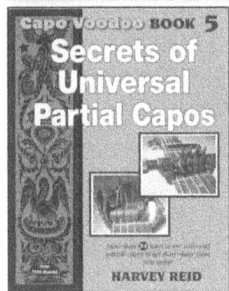

SECRETS OF UNIVERSAL PARTIAL CAPOS 45 ways to get new music from your guitar that can only be done with universal partial capos. This hidden world of music in your fingerboard includes a number of tunings and combinations with other partial capos. Over 1200 chords. Packed with photos, clear explanations and capo strategy will save you years of searching.

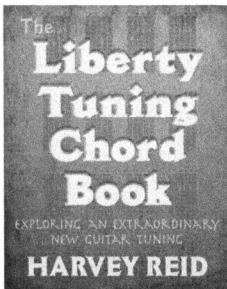

THE LIBERTY TUNING CHORD BOOK (2013) In his partial capo research, Harvey Reid discovered a simple new guitar tuning that introduces a remarkable geometrical symmetry and simplicity to the guitar fingerboard that no one ever dreamed existed. Here is a thorough examination of what this amazing tuning can do, with over 1200 chords, sorted, mapped out and organized to help you find your way in *Liberty Tuning*. Lots of tips, advice & clear explanations. For guitar teachers, beginners and anyone who already plays guitar and wants to learn about this important discovery.

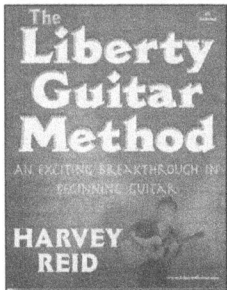

THE LIBERTY GUITAR METHOD (2013) Total beginners can play music like never before. It's easy to do and sounds great. Learn to use *Liberty Tuning* to play great-sounding, simple 2-finger chords to songs by Bob Dylan, Hank Williams, John Prine, Johnny Cash, Chuck Berry, The Beatles, Adele, and more. You won't believe it 'til you try it. *Hush Little Baby, This Land is Your Land, Your Cheating Heart, A Hard Rain's A Gonna Fall, Amazing Grace, The Cuckoo, Folsom Prison Blues, Angel From Montgomery, Maybellene, Let It Be, Imagine, Someone Like You, The Wedding Song, House of the Rising Sun*

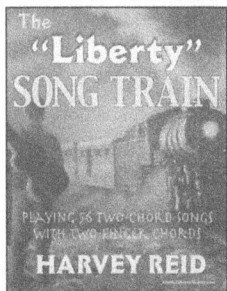

THE LIBERTY SONG TRAIN (2013) Learn how to use *Liberty Tuning* to play all 56 two-chord songs in the epic *Song Train* collection with just 2-finger chords, in the same keys as they were done on the *Song Train* recordings. Beginning guitar has never been easier. Careful explanations, with lots of helpful tips, strategy and advice. If you have the *Song Train* 4-CD collection, you need this companion book.

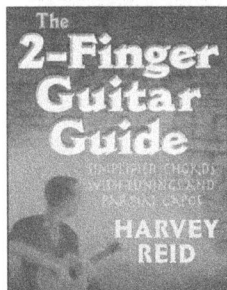

THE 2-FINGER GUITAR GUIDE (2013) A careful study of simplified guitar chords, this book takes you through each of the common tunings and partial capo configurations that can be used to play simplified guitar chords. Learn the advantages and disadvantages of each of 28 different guitar environments, including the amazing *Liberty Tuning* and related hybrid tunings. If you have a shortage of fingers on the fretting hand, or if you work with hand injuries, special music education or music therapy, this is the definitive guide to showing what can be done musically with just 2 finger chords.

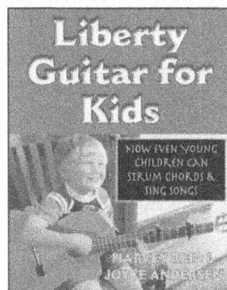

LIBERTY GUITAR FOR KIDS (2013) It's a huge breakthrough in children's guitar. Children as young as 4 can learn to strum simple 2-finger *Liberty Tuning* chords and play guitar like never before. Classic traditional plus modern children's songs arranged in keys young voices can sing in. No need to wait until the children grow bigger or waste your money on crummy small children's guitars. Learn how even small children can instantly start strumming songs on adult guitars. It's really amazing. *London Bridge, Row Row Row Your Boat, Farmer in the Dell, Hush Little Baby, This Land is Your Land, Oh Susannah, Standing in the Need of Prayer, Hey Lolly Lolly, Comin' Round the Mountain* and more.

ABOUT THE AUTHOR

Harvey Reid has been a full-time acoustic guitar player since 1974, and has performed over 6000 concerts throughout the US and in Europe. He won the 1981 *National Fingerpicking Guitar Competition* and the 1982 *International Autoharp* contest, and has released 28 highly-acclaimed recordings of original, traditional and contemporary acoustic music.

He is best known for his solo fingerstyle guitar work, but he is also a solid flatpicker (he won Bill Monroe's *Beanblossom* bluegrass guitar contest in 1976), a versatile singer, lyricist, prolific composer, arranger and songwriter. He also plays mandolin and bouzouki. Reid recorded the first album ever of 6 & 12-string banjo music, and his CD *Solo Guitar Sketchbook* made GUITAR PLAYER MAGAZINE's Top 20 essential acoustic guitar CD's list. His CD *Steel Drivin' Man* was chosen by ACOUSTIC GUITAR MAGAZINE as one of **Top 10 Folk CD's** of all time, along with Woody Guthrie, Ry Cooder and other hallowed names. His music was included in the blockbuster BBC TV show *A Musical Tour of Scotland*, and Reid was featured in the Rhino Records **Acoustic Music of the 90's** collection, along with a "who's who" line-up of other artists including Richard Thompson, Jerry Garcia & Leo Kottke.

In 1980 Reid published *A New Frontier in Guitar*, the first book about the partial capo, and in 1984 he wrote *Modern Folk Guitar*, the first college textbook for folk guitar. Quite possibly the first modern person to publish and record with the partial capo, he is almost certainly the most prolific arranger and composer of partial capo guitar music, and is responsible for most of what is known about the device. He lives in southern Maine with his family.